vanishing from WATERWAYS

by Gail Radley

illustrations by Jean Sherlock

Featuring poems by Jane Yolen, Lois Lenski, and others

Carolrhoda Books, Inc./Minneapolis

"Be infinitely tender and loving to animals." —*'Abdu'l-Bahá*
For my dear friends the Neiheisels—Robin, Bill, Philip, and especially Lauren—because they care.
—G. R.

The status of animals can change over time. To find out about an animal's current status, you can check this website: **<http://endangered.fws.gov/wildlife.html#species>**. For animals outside the United States, click on "Species Listed in Other Countries."

Photos are used courtesy of: p. 4, © Tom Bean; p. 5, Gerald and Buff Corsi/Focus on Nature, Inc.

Text copyright © 2001 by Gail Radley
Illustrations copyright © 2001 by Jean Sherlock

This book is available in two editions:
Library binding by Carolrhoda Books, Inc.,
  a division of Lerner Publishing Group
Soft cover by First Avenue Editions,
  an imprint of Lerner Publishing Group
241 First Avenue North
Minneapolis, MN 55401 U.S.A.

Website address: www.lernerbooks.com

Words in **bold type** are explained in a glossary on page 30.

Library of Congress Cataloging-in-Publication Data

Radley, Gail.
  Waterways / by Gail Radley; illustrations by Jean Sherlock.
    p. cm. — (Vanishing from)
  Includes index.
  Summary: Discusses through short essays and poems, ten endangered species that live in or along waterways, including scientific information about each, reasons for its endangered status, and descriptions of efforts to protect it.
  ISBN 1-57505-408-6 (lib. bdg. : alk. paper) ISBN 1-57505-569-4 (pbk. : alk. paper)
  1. Aquatic animals—Juvenile literature. 2. Endangered species—Juvenile literature. [1. Aquatic animals. 2. Endangered species.] I. Sherlock, Jean. II. Title. III. Series: Radley, Gail. Vanishing from.
QL122.2.R34 2001
591.76—dc21   97–28628

Manufactured in the United States of America
1 2 3 4 5 6 – JR – 06 05 04 03 02 01

Contents

4

Introduction

What would you do if the very last giant panda on earth was dying? You'd probably try to save it. Animals are dying out far more often than you might think. Scientists believe that about 50 **species,** or kinds, of animals die out each day. What's going on?

To understand, it might help to imagine all the pieces of a big jigsaw puzzle. Some pieces don't look important, and it's hard to see how they fit. But would you throw away those pieces? Of course not! You need them all to make a complete picture.

A giant elephant and a small white bird called a cattle egret help one another survive. The cattle egret eats insects on the elephant's skin. Besides grooming the elephant, the egret also acts as an alarm system, warning the elephant of approaching danger.

Our planet is a lot like a huge puzzle. The pieces come in different sizes. Some forms of life, such as bacteria, are very tiny. Others, like the mighty elephant or the towering redwood tree, are hard to miss.

Like puzzle pieces, all the living and nonliving things on the earth are connected. Some of the most important pieces of the puzzle combine to make up **habitats.** A habitat is the place where a plant or animal naturally lives. A habitat is made up of a mix of soil, air, water, weather, and living **organisms.**

The organisms in a habitat depend on each other to live. An **ecosystem** is the combination of organisms and their habitat. All ecosystems undergo change over time. Throughout history, changes in climate or habitat have made it more difficult for animals in an ecosystem to survive. When an ecosystem changes slowly, species have time to adapt. They can develop new traits to help them survive.

However, humans put many species in danger by making quicker changes to habitats. We cut down trees or grass so we can grow food or build houses. Humans also change environments by bringing in new plants and animals. The new species may compete with native species for food and space.

Humans use large amounts of natural resources. Water shortages and soil contamination change animal habitats. Hunting by humans has caused some species to die out and has pushed others in that direction. Laws to protect animals don't always help. Some animals have hides or other parts that are worth a lot of money. **Poachers**—people who hunt illegally—kill animals that are protected by law and sell their parts.

When the last member of an animal species dies, the species is **extinct.** Every animal that becomes extinct is a piece of the puzzle lost. And once that piece is gone, it's gone forever.

What's Being Done?

Scientists carefully watch animal populations. They call a species that's likely to become extinct **endangered.** **Threatened** creatures are not yet endangered, but their populations are shrinking. Some species fit into the **rare** category, meaning there have never been many of these creatures. A drop in a rare animal's population can push those creatures into the threatened group.

Ecologists make a recovery plan for animals in danger. They look at each creature's needs and think of ways to help meet those needs. Ecologists might suggest that lawmakers limit hunting of certain species. Sometimes scientists start a captive-breeding program. Wildlife experts capture threatened or endangered animals and take them to a zoo or a wildlife research center. Scientists hope the animals will be able to have babies and raise them in these safe places. If scientists believe the animals can survive in the wild, they may release some back into their natural habitat.

Scientists might recommend that land be set aside for a **wildlife refuge.** Here they maintain or restore habitats so that the land will support endangered, threatened, or rare creatures.

What Can You Do?

In *Waterways* you'll take a close look at 10 species in danger. As you read about these animals, think about how their stories make you feel. Do you feel sad? Or angry? Or happy that a species is doing better? A lot of people have written poems or essays to express their feelings about animals in danger. In this book, you will find a poem or other writing about each animal.

Reading about so many threatened animals can be overwhelming. You might think, "What could I possibly do that would make any difference?" Think again! Remember that big changes have to start somewhere. And they usually begin with small steps. To learn about what you can do to help, see the What You Can Do section on page 29.

KEY FACTS

STATUS:
Endangered

SCIENTIFIC NAME:
Egretta eulophotes

HISTORIC RANGE:
Breeding range includes China, Korea, and Russia; wintering grounds include the Philippines, Vietnam, and Thailand

SIZE:
Weighs 14 ounces; 27 inches long; wingspan 40 to 45 inches

DIET:
Fish, amphibians, small mammals, birds, insects, shrimp, crabs

LIFE SPAN:
17 years

Chinese Egret

Chinese egrets live in the shallow coastal waters of China and Korea. The birds grab fish with their long bills (beaks). This endangered species depends on mudflats—land covered part of the time by shallow ocean waters—for its survival. During the breeding season, egrets grow elaborate **plumes.** These long, soft feathers attract mates, but they also draw human hunters. In the late 1800s, hunters killed millions of egrets in China and Korea. Fashion designers used the plumes to decorate hats and clothing.

In 1922 conservationists created the International Council for Bird Preservation. The group worked to protect all bird species. Laws were passed against selling Chinese egret feathers. But the Chinese egret has not fully recovered from the heavy hunting.

Loss of habitat also threatens the birds. As people take over mudflats to raise crops or build houses, Chinese egrets have fewer places to live. Around 2,500 Chinese egrets survive throughout eastern Asia, but the birds are still dying at an alarming rate.

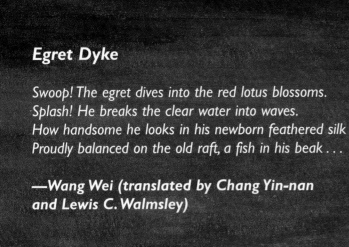

Egret Dyke

Swoop! The egret dives into the red lotus blossoms.
Splash! He breaks the clear water into waves.
How handsome he looks in his newborn feathered silk
Proudly balanced on the old raft, a fish in his beak . . .

—Wang Wei (translated by Chang Yin-nan
and Lewis C. Walmsley)

9

KEY FACTS

STATUS:
Endangered

SCIENTIFIC NAME:
Cyprinodon diabolis

HISTORIC RANGE:
Devil's Hole Cavern, Nevada

SIZE:
⅕ inch

DIET:
Algae

LIFE SPAN:
1 year

DEVIL'S HOLE Pupfish

It's amazing that anything can survive in an underground pond. But for the Devil's Hole pupfish, that is home. This fish lives only in Devil's Hole, a deep limestone cavern in southern Nevada. The pond is about 300 feet deep. Algae, tiny green plants that thrive in water, grow on a limestone shelf under the surface of the water. The Devil's Hole pupfish survives on this plant.

A drop in the water level means a drop in algae growth. So when ranchers dug several wells near Devil's Hole and began pumping out the underground water that supplied the pond, the tiny pupfish almost became extinct.

Conservationists declared the fish endangered in 1967. When the water level was too low for the algae to grow, scientists placed a fiberglass shelf in the water and shined light on it to encourage algae growth. This helped the pupfish population. In 1976 the U.S. Supreme Court limited the amount of water that could be pumped from the area. But Nevada ranchers need the water for their cattle. The survival of the Devil's Hole pupfish remains uncertain.

Devil's Hole Pupfish

In a single meadow,
A single pool:
Life.

Thumbnail fish,
Flitting through clear water
That bubbles from
Limestone caverns
Far below.

Flash of shining blue,
Splinter of yellow-brown:
Life.

Insistent.

—Gail Radley

KEY FACTS

STATUS:
Endangered

SCIENTIFIC NAME:
Monachus schauinslandi

HISTORIC RANGE:
Northwestern Hawaiian Islands

SIZE:
6½ feet long; weighs up to 330 pounds

LIFE SPAN:
30 years

HAWAIIAN Monk Seal

The Hawaiian monk seal lives only in Hawaii. Monk seals are playful creatures that can dive nearly 600 feet deep and can stay underwater for up to 20 minutes. If left alone, Hawaiian monk seals can live to be 30 years old. But more often than not, the seals die at a much younger age.

In the 1800s, hunters killed thousands of seals for their oil and skin. Hunting the seals has been against the law since the early 1970s. But the very presence of people on islands that were once deserted scares the seals away from their natural habitat. Hawaiian monk seals are also threatened by tiger sharks and fishing lines and nets. The fishing industry has greatly decreased the monk seal's food supply.

Declared endangered in 1976, Hawaiian monk seals are protected in the Hawaiian Islands National Wildlife Refuge. People who find monk seals on the beach must leave them alone. If a seal looks injured, people must report the seal's location. Scientists hope that these efforts will help increase the seal population.

Jewel

If it had been a sequin
it could not shine more bright,
a head of diamond could reflect
no sharper flash of light.
The seal looked this way and then that,
sparkling like early dew,
and then beneath the criss-cross waves
most silently withdrew.

—Elizabeth Coatsworth

13

African Slender-snouted Crocodile

KEY FACTS

STATUS:
Endangered

SCIENTIFIC NAME:
Crocodylus cataphractus

HISTORIC RANGE:
Western and central Africa

SIZE:
10 to 13 feet long; average weight unknown

DIET:
Crabs, fish, frogs, insects, shrimp, and snakes

LIFE SPAN:
40 to 50 years

In the shallow rivers of central and western Africa, endangered slender-snouted crocodiles drift near the surface like logs. But the crocodile can also go completely underwater. Except for round, glowing eyes, the crocodile is then hidden from sight. The creature can close its nostrils and ears and remain underwater for up to an hour.

The slender-snouted crocodile has few predators, because it moves quickly on land and in water. But throughout history, humans have hunted crocodiles for their meat.

Little is known about the status of the African slender-snouted crocodile. In some parts of its western African home, the crocodile is very rare. Laws have been passed against hunting the animal, but people are seldom caught or punished for breaking the laws. In some areas, hunting the crocodile is still permitted. Wars in West African countries also affect the protection of the crocodile. People fighting wars are less likely to follow laws that protect an animal. Poaching continues, and the African slender-snouted crocodile remains endangered.

From *Old Praise Song of the Crocodile*

The crocodile is the invoker of the waters of rain
The black one of the pool
The black black one lying on the water slime
It is the crocodile of the pool . . .

—Ancient African song from the Northern Sotho

15

KEY *FACTS*

STATUS:
Endangered

SCIENTIFIC NAME:
Megaptera
novaeangliae

HISTORIC RANGE:
Atlantic Ocean,
Pacific Ocean,
Indian Ocean,
Arctic Ocean

SIZE:
Averages 45 feet
long; weighs from
25 to 48 tons

DIET:
Mainly krill (tiny
shrimplike
animals) and fish,
including herring,
haddock,
mackerel, pollock

LIFE SPAN:
Up to 77 years

Humpback Whale

Humpback whales are huge—most grow to be about 45 feet long. But these playful creatures are able to leap gracefully above the ocean surface. They thump the water several times with their flat tails and then go back under.

In the past, whalers have hunted this slow swimmer. Between 1805 and 1907, American whalers killed at least 42,000 humpbacks. The animals were valued for their oil and baleen, and whale oil was used for fuel and cosmetics. Baleen is a set of strips of flexible bone in the whale's mouth that helps the whale strain food from the water. Baleen was used to make buggy whips and corsets.

In 1970 conservationists listed the humpback as endangered. Commercial hunting of the whale was banned. Since then, the number of humpbacks has increased to about 7,000 in U.S. waters. But the humpback whale is not completely out of danger. Conservationists are trying to reduce other threats to the humpback whale population. These threats include water pollution, fishing nets (in which whales can become entangled), collisions with ships as the whales **migrate,** and competition with people for food.

The Song of the Whale

Heaving mountain in the sea,
Whale, I heard you
Grieving.

Great whale, crying for your life,
Crying for your kind, I knew
How we would use
Your dying:

Lipstick for our painted faces,
Polish for our shoes.

Tumbling mountain in the sea,
Whale, I heard you
Calling. . . .

In the forest of the sea,
Whale, I heard you
Singing.

Singing to your kind.
We'll never let you be.
Instead of life we choose

Lipstick for our painted faces,
Polish for our shoes.

—Kit Wright

CHINOOK Salmon

Just before they die, chinook salmon swim from the Pacific Ocean back up the Columbia, Rogue, or Snake Rivers to where they were born. This journey takes months and can be up to 2,000 miles! The salmon swim against strong river currents and leap up waterfalls along the way. Salmon depend on this trip for the survival of their species. When they reach their birthplace, the fish **spawn,** or lay eggs.

Humans have changed the salmon's habitat by building dams to generate electricity. The dams stop many salmon from reaching their spawning grounds. Some salmon get caught in the equipment. Dams create pools of water called **reservoirs.** Reservoirs slow down and confuse the chinook. Water pollution, logging, and mining have also killed many chinook.

The United States National Marine Fisheries Service (NMFS) is considering removing four big dams on the Snake River. But many farmers depend on the dammed water for irrigation. The future of the chinook salmon still hangs in the balance.

Pacific Salmon

Bear teaser,
falls jumper,
autumn star
flashing silver
'til the spawning grounds
prove your eclipse.

—Jane Yolen

HAWKSBILL Sea Turtle

KEY FACTS

STATUS:
Endangered

SCIENTIFIC NAME:
Eretmochelys imbricata

HISTORIC RANGE:
Tropical reef areas of the Atlantic, Pacific, and Indian Oceans

SIZE:
Weighs up to 250 pounds; shell up to 3 feet long

DIET:
Sponges, mollusks, lobsters, crabs, jellies, and algae

LIFE SPAN:
Over 20 years (in captivity)

The hawksbill sea turtle glides along tropical reefs in the Atlantic, Pacific, and Indian Oceans. Between April and November, female hawksbills search for a beach on which to lay their eggs. Each female lays up to 150 eggs, covers them with sand, and then returns to the sea.

Unfortunately, many eggs will be destroyed or stolen before they can hatch. People drive off-road vehicles on some beaches, sometimes crushing the eggs. People also steal the eggs and eat them. Hawksbills that hatch and survive face other threats. Humans hunt the turtles for their beautiful shells, which are made into jewelry, combs, and frames for eyeglasses. People buy stuffed hawksbills to hang on their walls.

Since 1970 the hawksbill sea turtle has been protected in the United States. In Hawaii, it is against the law to sell turtle products. In other parts of the world, poachers can still make a lot of money selling the turtle shells. To protect the hawksbill, many countries have banned egg gathering and the buying of turtles or products made from them. But the turtles remain at risk.

KEY FACTS

STATUS:
Endangered

SCIENTIFIC NAME:
Trichechus manatus

HISTORIC RANGE:
Southeastern United States and Central America

SIZE:
Up to 12 feet long; weighs up to 3,500 pounds

DIET:
Aquatic plants

LIFESPAN:
50 to 60 years

WEST INDIAN Manatee

West Indian manatees graze in warm, shallow coastal waters of the southeastern United States and Central America. These gentle giants ride the currents, often playing follow-the-leader with other manatees. When sailors first saw manatees in the late 1500s, they thought they had seen mermaids.

In recent years, manatees have been forced to share their habitat with more and more motorboats. Boats' propellers sometimes hit manatees and injure them. Most manatees have scars from run-ins with boat propellers. Sometimes manatees don't survive a boat collision. One-fourth of manatee deaths in Florida are caused by boating accidents. Manatees face other dangers, including fishing nets, illegal hunting, and entrapment in floodgates and locks.

In 1978 Florida passed the Manatee Sanctuary Act, which established the entire state as a refuge for manatees. People who kill or disturb manatees must pay heavy fines. The law also allows enforcement of speed limits for boats in manatee areas. The manatee's survival depends on the protection of these laws.

From *Manatee*

Warm ocean or a quiet bay
   will lull this gentle giant
As she lolls and rolls to sway
   among the many grasses of the sea.
Contented Manatee.
   Grazing, gracing languidly
In underwater fields of weed,
   munching leisurely
With little need.

Sacred Seacow,
   Lover of the temperate sea,
Mermaid to the Ancients.
   Wallowing in shallow shores,
Ocean reefs and coral floors.
   Friendly Manatee,
Asks nothing of our earth
   but to browse and nibble water greens.
Our legendary Siren of the Sea,
   Peaceful Manatee.

—Jill Morgan Hawkins

KEY **FACTS**

STATUS:
Endangered

SCIENTIFIC NAME:
Ciconia boyciana

HISTORIC RANGE:
Breeds in China
and Russia;
winters in China,
Hong Kong, Japan,
North Korea,
South Korea, and
Taiwan

SIZE:
Up to 39 inches
long, with a
wingspan of 67
inches; weighs
almost 2 pounds

DIET:
Mainly frogs,
mice, lizards, fish,
and insects

LIFE SPAN:
Up to 48 years
(in captivity)

ORIENTAL White Stork

In Japan the Oriental white stork is believed to bring good luck. These elegant birds wade in marshes and rice fields, fishing for their favorite foods—fish, frogs, insects, and snails. Before 1970 the storks were common throughout China, Japan, North Korea, South Korea, and Russia.

Many events have led to the stork's decline. For years, poachers hunted the bird for its meat and bones, which people made into chopsticks. As more and more farmers began using chemicals to kill weeds and insects, those chemicals polluted the lakes. The fish that Oriental white storks eat the most died off. So the storks left areas, such as Japan, where they could no longer find food.

The last wild stork in Japan died in 1971. In an effort to reintroduce the stork, Japan opened the Hyogo Prefectural Homeland. At the 400-acre park, located in Toyooka City, scientists breed the storks and train them before returning them to the wild. Breeding has been somewhat successful. But as the bird's habitat continues to disappear, the Oriental white stork remains in danger.

As the stately stork,
    Standing, flaps his snowy wings
    In the bright sunlight,
On the tips of cherry-spray
    How delightfully blossoms sway!

—**Okamoto Kanoko**

25

KEY FACTS

STATUS:
Endangered

SCIENTIFIC NAME:
Pelecanus occidentalis

HISTORIC RANGE:
United States (California; North Carolina to Texas), Mexico, South America (Brazil, Chile, Venezuela and Guyana), and islands in the Caribbean Sea

SIZE:
42 to 54 inches long, with a wingspan of up to 7½ feet; weighs 8 to 10 pounds

DIET:
Fish, lobsters, and other shellfish

LIFE SPAN:
30 years or more

BROWN Pelican

From 50 feet above the ocean waves, the brown pelican spots a fish. The bird dives into the water and scoops up the fish in its long, straight bill. Under its bill, the pelican has a pouch that expands to hold water or fish. When the brown pelican resurfaces, it may be holding up to three gallons of water in its pouch. The bird lets the water run out, then tips its head back to swallow the fish.

Fish are the brown pelican's favorite food. But in the 1950s, the fish in the pelican's habitat became unsafe to eat. They contained DDT, a chemical that farmers then used to kill insects. DDT had seeped into rivers, lakes, and oceans. Pelicans that ate poisoned fish laid eggs with very thin shells. The eggs often broke before young pelicans could hatch. By the early 1960s, brown pelicans had nearly disappeared from the United States.

In 1972 DDT was banned in the United States, and other harmful pesticides were restricted. The pelican population is slowly recovering—about 6,000 breeding pairs live along the Gulf Coast. But the brown pelican remains endangered in several areas.

Pelican

Wise old pelican
bunched on a stump
watching and waiting
ready to jump.

Huge old bill
big deep pouch
sits there sleeping—
mean old grouch.

Hunger gnaws
fisherman baiting
pelican turns
tired of waiting.

Fish leaps up—
gone in a flash
pelican swallows
makes a big splash.

Wings out-spread
back to the stump
to watch and wait
ready to jump.

Fish is gone
pelican winks—
Nobody knows
what he thinks.

—Lois Lenski

27

Map of Animal Ranges

ARCTIC
OCEAN

ARCTIC
OCEAN

NORTH
AMERICA

EUROPE

ASIA

ATLANTIC
OCEAN

AFRICA

PACIFIC
OCEAN

Hawaii (U.S.)

SOUTH
AMERICA

INDIAN
OCEAN

AUSTRALIA

PACIFIC
OCEAN

- Chinese egret
- Devil's Hole pupfish
- Brown pelican
- Hawaiian monk seal
- Hawksbill sea turtle**
- Oriental white stork
- Humpback whale*
- West Indian manatee
- Chinook salmon
- African slender-snouted crocodile

*found in all the oceans   **found in tropical reefs in Atlantic, Pacific, and Indian Oceans

What You Can Do

The problem of species in danger may seem too big to tackle. But the efforts of many concerned people have saved some creatures from extinction. There are lots of things that young people can do to help.

Educate yourself.

- *Read books, nature magazines, and newspaper articles to learn about the animals. Then share your knowledge. When you spread the word about an animal in danger, you'll find that other people may want to help.*

- *Discuss a book about endangered animals for your next book report.*

- *Create a class scrapbook with pictures of each student's favorite endangered species.*

- *Create a save-the-animals bulletin board at school.*

- *Make informative buttons to wear on clothes or backpacks.*

- *Ask your teacher to arrange for a local conservationist to talk to your class.*

Take action.

- *Join a conservation club. People in these groups work to educate the public about endangered animals and their habitats.*

- *Encourage people not to buy products made from wild animal parts.*

- *When your parents are buying furniture or other products, ask if they'll shop around until they find ecosystem-friendly items.*

Help animals before they become threatened or endangered.

- *Set up a feeder for migratory birds.*

- *Help reduce air pollution—bike, walk, bus, or carpool.*

- *Pitch in on local clean-up days and encourage people not to litter.*

Decrease the amount of garbage your family or school produces.

- *Recycle glass, metal, paper, and plastic.*

- *Buy products made from recycled materials and shop at secondhand stores.*

- *"Precycle"—buy products that use the least packaging, such as food in bulk bins.*

For More Information

The following organizations have more tips on what you can do to help endangered wildlife:

National Audubon Society, 700 Broadway • New York, NY 10003 www.audubon.org

National Wildlife Federation, 8925 Leesburg Pike • Vienna, VA 22184 www.nwf.org

Sierra Club, 85 Second Street, Second Floor • San Francisco, CA 94105 www.sierraclub.org

World Wildlife Fund/Conservation Foundation, Education Department • 1250 24th Street NW • Washington, D.C. 20037 www.worldwildlife.org

Glossary

ecosystem: a carefully balanced community of soil, air, water, climate, and organisms

endangered: a category used by conservationists to describe species that are in danger of becoming extinct

extinct: a category used by scientists to describe a species that has died out

habitat: the place or environment where a plant or animal naturally lives

migrate: to move from one region to another when the season changes

organism: any living thing

plume: a large fluffy feather

poacher: a person who hunts wildlife illegally

rare: a category used by conservationists to describe species with small but stable populations that require careful watch

reservoir: a place where water is collected and stored for later use

spawn: to produce young in large numbers, especially by aquatic (water) animals, such as fish

species: the basic groups into which scientists classify animals. Animals of the same species share traits that make them different from all other life-forms.

threatened: a category used by conservationists to describe species that are in less danger than those in the endangered group but that are likely to move toward extinction if present conditions continue

wildlife refuge: land set aside as a shelter on which wildlife can safely live

Further Reading

Cerfolli, Fulvio. *Adapting to the Environment.* Austin, TX: Raintree Steck-Vaughn, 1999.

Harrison, Michael, and Christopher Stuart-Clark. *Oxford Book of Animal Poems.* New York: Oxford University Press, 1992.

Hirschi, Ron. *Salmon.* Minneapolis: Carolrhoda Books, 2001.

Patent, Dorothy Hinshaw. *Back to the Wild.* San Diego: Gulliver Books, 1997.

Relf, Patricia. *Magic School Bus Hops Home: A Book about Animal Habitats.* New York: Scholastic, 1995.

Staub, Frank. *Manatees.* Minneapolis: Lerner Publications Company, 1998.

Vergoth, Karin, and Christopher Lampton. *Endangered Species.* New York: Franklin Watts, 1999.

Woodward, John. *Crocodiles & Alligators.* New York: Benchmark Books, 1999.

Index Numbers in **bold** refer to photos and illustrations

About the Author and Illustrator

Gail Radley has published nearly two dozen books. An animal lover, she's concerned about the large number of species whose survival is in danger. Radley lives with her husband, Joe, daughter, Jana, and their schnauzer, Toby, in DeLand, Florida. She is a lecturer in the English department at Stetson University.

Illustrator Jean Sherlock has long been combining her love of wildlife and her artistic talents. Her nature illustrations first appeared in publications while she was still in her early teens. Jean's other interests include fishing, bird-watching, and falconry. She and her red-tailed hawk enjoy hunting excursions throughout the United States.

Poetry Acknowledgments

The poems included in *Waterways* are reprinted by permission of the following: p. 9, "Egret Dyke" by Wang Wei. The author has made every effort to obtain permission to use "Egret Dyke"; p. 11, "Devil's Hole Pupfish" by Gail Radley; p. 13, "Jewel" reprinted by permission of Simon & Schuster Books for Young Readers, an imprint of Simon & Schuster Children's Publishing Division, copyright © 1948 Macmillan Publishing Company; copyright renewed © 1976, Elizabeth Coatsworth Beston; p. 15, "Old Praise Song of the Crocodile" by S. K. Lekgothani, from *Bantu Studies XII*, reprinted by permission of Witwatersrand University Press; p. 17, "The Song of the Whale" (p. 17, 20 lines) from *Hot Dog and Other Poems* by Kit Wright (Kestrel Books, 1981) copyright © Kit Wright, 1981. Reprinted by permission of Penguin Books, Ltd; p. 19, "Pacific Salmon" copyright © 1996 by Jane Yolen from *Sea Watch*, published by Philomel Books, reprinted by permission of both Putnam and Curtis Brown, Ltd.; p. 21, "Sea Turtle" from *Summer Green* by Elizabeth Coatsworth. Reprinted by permission of Kegan Paul International, London, U.K.; p. 23, "Manatee" printed by permission of Jill Morgan Hawkins; p. 25, "As the stately stork" by Okamoto Kanoko. The author has made every effort to obtain permission to use "As the stately stork"; p. 27, "Pelican" by Lois Lenski from *Florida My Florida* by Lois Lenski, Florida State University, 1971, reprinted by permission of Lois Lenski, Covey Foundation Inc.